Beyoncé

ABDO
Publishing Company

A Big Buddy Book
by **Sarah Tieck**

VISIT US AT
www.abdopublishing.com

Published by ABDO Publishing Company, 8000 West 78th Street, Edina, Minnesota 55439.

Copyright © 2009 by Abdo Consulting Group, Inc. International copyrights reserved in all countries. No part of this book may be reproduced in any form without written permission from the publisher. Buddy Books™ is a trademark and logo of ABDO Publishing Company.

Printed in the United States of America, North Mankato, Minnesota.
012009
012012

Coordinating Series Editor: Rochelle Baltzer
Contributing Editors: Heidi M.D. Elston, Megan M. Gunderson, Marcia Zappa
Graphic Design: Maria Hosley
Cover Photograph: AP Photo: Chris Pizzello
Interior Photographs/Illustrations: AP Photo: Tammie Arroyo (page 18), Jeff Christensen (page 25), Jim Cooper (page 19), Kevork Djansezian (page 13), Richard Drew (page 23), Electronic City Entertainment/Nepathya (page 11), Jennifer Graylock (page 7), Imaginechina via AP Images (page 29), Julie Jacobson (page 26), Hermann J. Knippertz (page 21), Bill Kostroun (page 26), Nekesa Moody (page 6), Chris Pizzello (pages 5, 25), Mark J. Terrill (page 21); Getty Images: AMA/Getty Images for AMA/Frank Micelotta (page 8), ImageDirect/Tim Mosenfelder (page 15), WireImage/Jim Smeal (page 17).

Library of Congress Cataloging-in-Publication Data

Tieck, Sarah, 1976-
  Beyoncé / Sarah Tieck.
     p. cm. -- (Big buddy biographies)
  Includes index.
  ISBN 978-1-60453-117-6
  1. Knowles, Beyoncé--Juvenile literature. 2. Singers--United States--Biography--Juvenile literature. I. Title.

ML3930.K66T54 2008
782.42164092--dc22
[B]
                              2008010462

Beyoncé

Contents

Singing Star

Beyoncé Knowles is a famous singer and actress. She has made award-winning albums. And, she has starred in successful movies.

Beyoncé was in the popular music group Destiny's Child.

Solange also sings and acts.

Family Ties

Beyoncé Giselle Knowles was born in Houston, Texas, on September 4, 1981. Her parents are Tina and Mathew Knowles. Beyoncé has one younger sister named Solange.

6

The Knowles family likes to help others.
Mathew and Tina often attend charity events.

The Knowles family worked hard to help Beyoncé become a successful singer. Their hard work paid off!

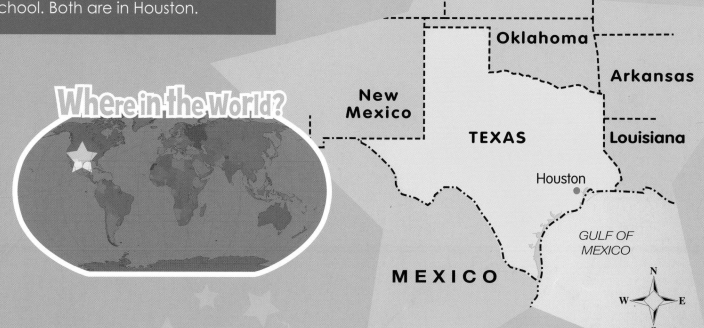

Where in the World?

Oklahoma

Arkansas

New Mexico

TEXAS

Louisiana

Houston

GULF OF MEXICO

MEXICO

Beyoncé grew up in a large house in Houston. Her father was a successful salesman. Her mother owned a popular hair salon.

Early Years

As a young girl, Beyoncé sang in choirs at school and church. She also took dance lessons. When Beyoncé was seven, she won the first of many talent **competitions**. People soon noticed her gift for singing.

Did you know...

Before Beyoncé started performing, she was shy. So on stage, Beyoncé sometimes pretends she is someone else. This trick makes it easier to perform.

Beyoncé won more than 30 talent competitions! She especially moved one crowd when she sang "Imagine" by John Lennon.

Starting Out

In 1992, Beyoncé, Kelly Rowland, and LaTavia Roberson were part of a music group. It was called Girl's Tyme. The girls practiced singing, dancing, and rapping for hours each day.

Later that year, Girl's Tyme was chosen to **compete** on *Star Search*. The girls thought this would be their big break. But, they did not win.

Beyoncé and Kelly are cousins.
They are also close friends.

13

Destiny's Child first became known in 1998. The group included LaTavia, Beyoncé, Kelly, and LeToya.

After *Star Search*, Girl's Tyme performed at many events. They became known for their **rhythm and blues**, pop, and rap sound.

Mathew left his sales job to **manage** the struggling group. Soon LeToya Luckett joined the group. After several name changes, Girl's Tyme became Destiny's Child.

Rising Stars

Destiny's Child worked very hard. In 1998, the group **released** its first album. It is called *Destiny's Child*. One year later, the girls released their second album. It is titled *The Writing's on the Wall*. Both albums were popular and sold well.

Two well-known songs by Destiny's Child are "Say My Name" and "Jumpin', Jumpin'."

In 2000, Destiny's Child changed. After a disagreement, some members left. And, new members joined. In the end, the group included Beyoncé, Kelly, and Michelle Williams.

The new group **released** two more albums. After a couple of years, they decided to split up. In 2005, Destiny's Child performed around the world in a farewell tour.

Did you know...

In 2002, Beyoncé was the first African-American woman named Songwriter of the Year by the American Society of Composers, Authors and Publishers.

In 2001, Destiny's Child won a Grammy Award for "Say My Name." This is a big honor for musicians.

New Opportunities

In 2003, Beyoncé **released** her first **solo** album. It is called *Dangerously In Love*. The album was very popular with fans.

In 2004, Beyoncé won five Grammy Awards for *Dangerously In Love*. This tied the record set for most wins for a single female artist in one night.

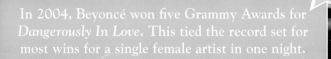

Did you know...

B'Day was released on Beyoncé's twenty-fifth birthday.

B'Day is Beyoncé's second album. It was **released** in 2006. This popular album received a **Grammy Award**. Later, Beyoncé recorded some of the album's songs for a Spanish album.

Beyoncé's music has made her famous. She has appeared on magazine covers. Also, she has been **interviewed** on television shows, such as *The Oprah Winfrey Show*.

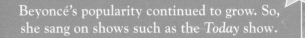

Beyoncé's popularity continued to grow. So, she sang on shows such as the *Today* show.

Movie Star

Beyoncé is a talented actress, too. Her first big **role** was in 2002. She appeared in *Austin Powers in Goldmember*.

In 2006, Beyoncé acted in *The Pink Panther*. That same year, she starred in *Dreamgirls*.

DREAMGIRLS

Dreamgirls tells the story of a singer's rise to fame.

In *Austin Powers in Goldmember*, Beyoncé played Foxxy Cleopatra. She worked with actors Mike Myers *(bottom middle)*, Michael Caine *(middle right)*, and Verne Troyer *(bottom right)*.

Jay-Z and Beyoncé often watch
New Jersey Nets basketball games.
Jay-Z is one of the team's owners.

In 2003, Beyoncé and Jay-Z
performed "Crazy in Love" at the
MTV Video Music Awards.

Off the Stage

Beyoncé began dating rapper Jay-Z in 2002. They share a strong love of music. Jay-Z has performed on some of Beyoncé's albums. And, he has helped her write some songs.

Beyoncé and Jay-Z were married April 4, 2008. They live in New York City, New York.

Buzz

Beyoncé's opportunities continue to grow and change. She records new songs in Spanish.

In 2008, Beyoncé acted in the movie *Cadillac Records*. In it, she plays famous singer Etta James. Fans are excited to see what's next for Beyoncé Knowles.

Most of Beyoncé's music is rhythm and blues. But, *B'Day* has more dance songs.

Snapshot

⭐ **Name**: Beyoncé Giselle Knowles

⭐ **Birthday**: September 4, 1981

⭐ **Birthplace**: Houston, Texas

⭐ **Home**: New York City, New York

⭐ **Musical groups**: Girl's Tyme, Destiny's Child

⭐ **Solo albums**: *Dangerously In Love, B'Day*

⭐ **Appearances**: *Austin Powers in Goldmember, The Pink Panther, Dreamgirls, Cadillac Records*

Important Words

competition a contest between two or more persons or groups.

Grammy Award any of the more than 100 awards given each year by the National Academy of Recording Arts and Sciences. Grammy Awards honor the year's best accomplishments in music.

interview to ask someone a series of questions.

manage to direct the work of a person or a group.

release to make available to the public.

rhythm (RIH-thuhm) **and blues** a form of popular music that features a strong beat. It is inspired by jazz, gospel, and blues styles.

role a part an actor plays in a show.

solo a performance by a single person.

Web Sites

To learn more about Beyoncé, visit ABDO Publishing Company on the World Wide Web. Web sites about Beyoncé are featured on our Book Links page. These links are routinely monitored and updated to provide the most current information available.

www.abdopublishing.com

Index